The Little Book of
Neds

Whit ye lookin at, ya muppet?

D0928420

Crombie Jardine
PUBLISHING LIMITED

Unit 17, 196 Rose Street, Edinburgh EH2 4AT
www.crombiejardine.com

This edition was first published by
Crombie Jardine Publishing Limited in 2005

1st reprint, 2005

ISBN 1-905102-30-5

Compiled by Julie Davidson and Crombie Jardine
Illustrations by Helen West and Rob Smith
Designed by www.mrstiffy.co.uk
Printed & Bound in Great Britain by
William Clowes Ltd, Beccles, Suffolk

Contents

Introduction

In 2004 I wrote a book called *The Little Book of Chavs*. Little did I know that the whole country would be going Chav mad. In January that year nobody had heard of Chavs but by December everyone had!

In *The Little Book of Chavs* I invited readers to email me with their comments. The one area I got the most emails from was Scotland, where Chavs go by the name of Neds. I decided that there was nothing else for it but to take the high road and spend some time in Scotland and research this distinctly Scottish branch of Chavdom.

Glasgow has a long history of gang warfare with group names

like The Billy Boys, Tongs,
The Monks and The Ruehill
Boys all part of the culture.
Nowhere else in Britain are
the Neds so gang-minded, with
posses of them from places like
Maryhill, Easterhouse and Milton
regularly fighting each other.

Lastly – and because I said I
would – I want to thank the
Neds I spent a few hours with
in Glasgow; this book would
have been a lot harder to write

without the help of Malkie,
wee Shug and Jamesie.
Thanks, guys!

If you have any comments, please
email me at neds@crombiejardine.
com. Anything interesting will be
added to future editions.

Lee Bok

Chapter 1

What is a Ned?

The word Ned is traditionally a Glaswegian term, meaning a young layabout or thug. In the east of Scotland, Neds have sometimes been described as Gadges or Schemies (as in Housing Scheme), and in England they are most commonly referred to as Chavs.

Nowadays, Ned is a word used throughout Scotland to describe a young (usually) male Burberry-clad, foul-mouthed yob, the likes of whom can be seen up and down the country.

Some claim that the word is an acronym for Non-Educated [sic] Delinquent, however, this seems unlikely, apart from being ungrammatical. This acronym theory most probably stems from Rosie Kane MSP, who famously stood up for Neds in the Scottish Parliament, stating that, 'The term 'ned' is hurtful and disrespectful to young people'. Was this a cynical ploy to gain the Ned vote? If so, I fear Ms Kane was disappointed, as most Neds over the age of 18 don't even know what an MSP is, never mind what voting is all about.

Another theory doing the rounds is that the term Ned is short for Edward, as in Teddy Boy.

Yet another theory – and this
one has legs, for sure! – is that
Ned comes from the old Scots
word for donkey (Neddy): Neds
start each statement with
an 'Eeeeeeeeey' sound which
resembles a donkey braying.

Even if you have never seen a Ned,
you will have seen their names and
gang slogans scrawled on walls,
on the back of bus seats, at bus
shelters, on the back of toilet doors
in pubs or MacDonald's, etc. – all

scratched with a 2p coin.

Anyone who has met a lone Ned will know that they are actually fairly friendly and pleasant people – when they're on their own. It is only in the presence of a fellow Ned, or audience of Neds, that they undergo the Jekyll and Hyde transformation into the creatures we have come to know so well.

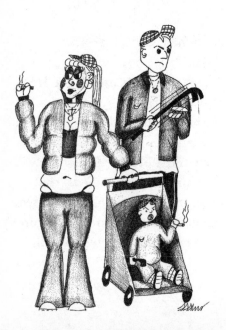

Chapter 2

A History of Neds

Before we had Neds, we had:

TEDDY BOYS – 1940s and '50s

These Neds' clothing was inspired by Edwardian dress, combined with the American trends of the time. So instead of the now infamous white tracksuit, Teddy Boys wore long jackets that sloped off the shoulders, and sported extra-large cuffs. This look was polished off with drainpipe trousers that were thought rather risqué at the time. In place of a Burberry cap, Teddy Boys took great pride in their hair, teasing and lacquering it lovingly with Brylcreem into an outrageous quiff with a DA (duck's arse) at the back.

By all accounts, these Teddy Boys terrorized the streets of Scotland – in a similar way to our modern day, logo-loving Neds – hanging about drinking in the dancehalls, causing trouble and fuelling reports of razor-blade carrying gangs.

MODS AND ROCKERS – 1960s

The Mods and Rockers were opposing gangs, like Celtic and Rangers Neds are today. However, the difference was not just in the name of the team emblazoned on their shirt. It was in the taste of music, the general lifestyle choices and the all-important status symbol... yes, you guess it – the wheels!

The Mods were the working class group, and, like Neds today, tried hard to dress in a fashion that shouted wealth. But the sharp suits and pointed shoes failed miserably to achieve that ever-elusive effect.

Like Sengas, Mod girls wore androgynous clothing. They were

associated with drug use and, like Neds, their 'motor' was all-important. Unfortunately for them, this usually took the form of a Vespa scooter...

The Rockers listened to Rock and Roll, and their uniform consisted of jeans, boots and leather jackets.

They took extraordinary pride in enhancing their prized motorcycles – in much the same way that modern-day Neds individualize their Novas.

However, there weren't many Mods
and Rockers in Scotland; they
tended to concentrate in Liverpool
and the south of England,
especially Brighton, where the
Mods and Rockers would beat the
shit out of each other for fun every
Bank Holiday.

SKINHEADS – 1970s and '80s

Named after their distinctive
bald-headed style, these Neds
were very much associated with

racism and Neo-Nazism. Instead of Timberland boots, a Skinhead would probably put on a pair of Doc Martins and go for punk rock over trance music any day.

These so-called Bovver Boys were named because wherever they went, bovver followed. Skinheads very commonly sported DIY tattoos and German Army surplus gear. Football hooliganism was a common occurrence for Skinheads, as it is for our Neds today.

Chapter 3

Ned Hotspots:

The Natural Habitat of the Ned

There is not a single town in Scotland with a population of more than three (Ned 1, Ned 2, and someone to pick on) that does not harbour a few Neds.

However, there are many places in the country that have a full-scale influx. Take Glasgow, for example...

Legend has it that it was actually Glasgow that spawned the first baseball-capped, tracksuit-wearing Ned within its boundaries.

For the hard-core Ned-spotting enthusiast, I would strongly advise a trip to Sauchiehall Street in

Glasgow at around 3pm
on a Saturday.

You know for certain that you have
Neds if the statues in your town
commonly sport rather dashing
traffic-cone headwear...

Armadale, West Lothian,
apparently has a heavy Ned
contingency. Neds can be seen
carrying a bottle of Buckfast

around with them, stopping
for a swig every few minutes.

Dundee, too, has an abundance
of Neds.

Inverness was thought to have
escaped the Ned influx unscathed
but I have it on good authority
that there ARE Neds in this neck
of the woods, but they are quite
gentlemanly in comparison to the

Sighthill Neds. Bless.

Other affected towns that have
come to attention are (in no
particular order):

Motherwell, Livingston, Paisley,
Dunfermline, Dundee, Glenrothes,
Greenock, Coatbridge, Stranraer,
Hamilton, Lanark, Bathgate,
North Berwick, Penicuik and
Airdrie, Stonehaven, Tobermory,

Renfrew, Inverbervie, Arbroath,
Forfar, Methil, Dunblane,
Dalkeith, Loanhead, Craigmiller,
Largs, Gourock, Grangemouth,
Aberdeen, Carstairs, Auchterarder,
Dunkeld, Pitlochry, Perth, Kinross,
Tomintoul, Elgin, Peterhead,
Turriff, Fraserburgh, Tayport,
Newport-on-Tay, Newburgh,
Anstruther, Kirkcaldy, Peebles...
and, despite the general consensus,
yes, Edinburgh DOES harbour
Neds, like it or not!

Within each town, there are several hotspots for Nedspotting. These include:

* Outside shopping precincts

* Outside bowling alleys

* The nearest stretch of straight road, to race their motors on

* Bus shelters

* Outside off-licences

* MacDonald's, Wimpy, KFC, Burger King or the local chippie

* Job Centres

* Social Security Offices

* Argos

* The Pound Shop

* Lidl

* Aldi.

The off-licence breed of Ned will
most likely have a 'dug' named
Killer or Tyson that s/he threatens
to 'set on ye' as you go to buy
a pint of milk. However, this
forlorn animal is invariably of the
Yorkshire terrier variety or similar,
and highly unlikely to cause any
major damage to you.

Chapter 4

The Senga

Like a herd of animals in nature,
every gang of Neds requires a
dominant matriarch figure. In
this society she is the Senga. This
name was given to many from the
previous generation of Neds, but
has somehow stuck.

The Senga is usually seen
wearing dirty white trainers with
grotesquely tight black trousers,
a prominent thong strap rising
well above them is a must, all
accompanied by a tiny strappy
top, with a sports jacket on top,
zipped only to navel level. The
look is accessorized with about
eight gold Argos earrings in
each ear, numerous gold chains
and medallions sinking into the
cleavage, and, of course, a Burberry
cap pointing skywards.

The ultimate fashion accessory for the Senga, though, is a pushchair. This is either filled with at least two sportswear-clad, dirty-faced 'weans' or with Lidl bags, with the kids trailing behind. It is usually possible to hear the Senga coming before she actually appears, with cries of 'Britney!!! Dinnae pull your skirt doon in the street!' or 'Dylan! Leave mammy's fags alone!!'

These Sengas commonly find their 15 minutes of fame on the TV chat show 'Trisha', hoping to prove that their bairn's father's brother is actually their bairn's sister's sister... Only to find that their father's brother's bairn's sister is actually their mother, by cunning use of DNA testing.

Sengas are typically either incredibly skinny, or grotesquely fat. We do not know what they do with the midsized members of their species. It is possible that they migrate to a kind of waste(or should that be waist)land for the intervening years.

Chapter 5

Ned Style

Neds are known for their characteristic tracksuit-and-trainers combo that is worn for all occasions under the sun. However, it is wrong to presume that every person wearing sports gear is a Ned; they may actually be going to play sport – something Neds rarely do, unless it involves kicking an empty drink can. A reliable way of identifying a genuine Ned is a glass bottle of Irn Bru sticking out of one pocket, and a rolled up Daily Star or Sport in the other.

Other Ned trends include:

Burberry

The distinctive Burberry pattern was once an exclusive brand for affluent countryside-types, perhaps worn to a polo match or displayed on a travel rug in the Range Rover.

Nowadays Burberry is banned in many bars and clubs, due to its reputation as a Ned favourite. Neds everywhere wear Burberry coats, Burberry bags, Burberry umbrellas, Burberry underwear, Burberry scarves, and, of course, the now famous Burberry cap.

It has to be said that, unfortunately for Burberry, the Neds-Burberry is not usually from the reputable store. Neds' pieces are more often than not brought back from European tourist resorts such as Ibiza, the Canary Islands and the Spanish Costa, where a fake-Burberry industry thrives.

Jewellery

No Ned is complete without his/her bit of bling! bling!

The Ned bling thing is usually in the form of at least six gold chains worn together in a messy tangle round the neck and thick fake-gold bracelets which double as knuckle-dusters, if the opportunity for a good fight comes along.

For females, the trick is to cram as many gold sovereign rings or as many of their mum's ex-wedding rings on each finger as possible. Also, it is considered stylish to wear a gold nametag necklace, the bigger the better. This is possibly a device to aid male Neds find the Senga they have previously arranged to spend the night with.

Any Argos store on a Saturday is a good place to spot Neds buying bling. However, buying real gold from a shop is only done by those Neds lucky enough to hold down a job.

Hairstyles

It is very rare to see a Ned without his/her Burberry cap.

However if you do find one, a male Ned will tend to have a very short hairstyle, often entirely bleached, or he may have a pattern or message written in bleach. It is also popular to have sports logos shaved into the back of the head.

Females either have their hair pulled back and moussed into a tight bun that has often been described as a 'council-house facelift', or tied back with fluorescent scrunches, and the lank ponytail put through the gap at the back of their Burberry cap. It is most commonly of a light orange colour, a sign of a botched home-bleaching attempt.

Footwear

When it comes to shoes, Neds have two options: trainers or Timberland boots.

The trainers are usually white, commonly laced up underneath the tongue, causing it to flap comically as the Ned walks. The socks are usually of the white sports variety, which are worn pulled up over the

bottom of the trousers. It is
not exactly clear why Neds do
this; it may be to stop a draught
coming up the trousers, or
to keep the dazzlingly white
tracky bottoms clean. The most
convincing theory is that it stops
the stolen goods that the Ned has
stuffed down his trousers from
falling out the bottom.

Timberland boots, referred to
as Timbies, are worn without laces,
so the Ned's foot lifts out of the

boot entirely as he legs it from the polis. These are usually of a light tan colour.

Ned Favourite Brands

Burberry

Buckfast

Timberland

Reebok

Nike

White Lightning

Von Dutch

Harvey's Bristol Cream

Louis Vuitton

Tiffany

Stone Island

Nickelson

Hackett

Nova

MD 20/20

Chapter 6

Ned Lingo

If a Ned yells any of these terms in your direction, it is prudent to leg it to prevent getting a sore face.

"Oi! Fannybaws!"
You there! Vagina-testicles.
(This gem's comedy genius is lost on the Neds who use it.)

"Yir a bawbag by the way."
Might I add that you are a scrotum.

"Ya wee prick."
It is my opinion that you are,
essentially, a small penis.

"I'll take the c*nt right oot ye!"
(Many theories abound as to what
this means exactly but none are
printable here.)

"Yir banter's pure pish."
You are not skilled in the art of good
conversation.

"Yir Maw."
Your mother.
(This is a standard response to
anything a Ned doesn't believe or
understand. For example, if you said
to a Ned, 'I saw yir burd get aff wi
wee Mikey', his immediate response
would most likely be, 'Aye, yir maw').

"I'll chib ye, ye fanny."
I am going to cause damage to you
with my weapon, you vagina.

"Yir a cock-jockey."
You regularly engage in
homosexual activities.

"Shut yir geggy, ye tube."
Refrain from speaking, you fool.

"Haw you! Whit ye lookin' at?"
Excuse me, what are you looking at?

"Yir a spoon."
Your mental acumen is well
below par.

"Ma Timbies are well better
than yours."
My Timberland boots are clearly
superior to your pair.

"Ya pure mad mento muppet."
You are one mad person.

"Haud your Weesh'd."
Be quiet for a minute, old boy.

"Get tae fuck!"
Go away, now!

"Haw ya bas!"
Hello, you bastard!

"Run, ya spoon, it's the polis."
Get a move on, my man, the
police are coming.

"I'm an animal in bed, ken."
(This is not aimed at his friend Ken.)
Do you know, I am great in bed.

"Are ye a goff?"
Do you dress in a gothic fashion?

Chapter 7

How to Insult A Ned

Although it can be sorely tempting, it is wise to ensure that there is a safe distance between you and the Ned before insulting him/her.

Here is a selection of the most cutting remarks:

* You could fit more rings on that finger.

* You're 12 and you don't have a bairn yet.

* Your jewellery isn't from Argos.

* You look very individual in
  that tracksuit.

* Your Granny is over 30.

* You look like a Goth.

* Your ma's so fat when I said it's chilly outside she went running with a spoon.

Chapter 8

Motors

Any Ned aged 17 or over must have a motor in order to gain and maintain that all-important status.

The most sought-after vehicle is almost always a Vauxhall Nova, or, for the more affluent Ned, a Vauxhall Corsa.

A true Ned will spend hours

tinkering with his (or her) pride and joy, and the more utterly unnecessary, ridiculous accessories fitted to it, the better.

Common additions are:

* Burberry seat covers.

* Furry dice.

* Go-faster stripes.

* Ironing board spoilers.

* Hub-caps made to look like alloy-

wheels, usually with a different design on each wheel.

* A huge sound system, consisting of at least two enormous, concert-sized speakers in the boot. A true Ned motor is always worth less than the sound-system it contains.

* An oversized exhaust, the purpose of which is to emulate the sound of a large engine. The obvious aim is to make the regular 900cc Nova sound like a Ferrari.

* The whole car is 'de-badged'.
  This involves removing all make
  and model badges. These are
  occasionally replaced by Celtic or
  dragon motifs, sprayed onto the
  bonnet or on the back. In the case
  of a Senga's motor, the Playboy
  symbol is commonly displayed.

* Under-car neon lighting is fitted.
  This makes the car appear to glow
  from underneath. Coming along a
  country lane late at night, the
  casual observer would be forgiven

for thinking that they have sighted a UFO -- especially if they have caught sight of the occupant at the wheel.

* Darkened glass is fitted. This has two functions: the Ned can avoid identification by the polis if caught speeding; and the motor can easily be used as a portable bedroom if the Ned finds a willing Senga.

Chapter 9

Bevvies

In order to choose an alcoholic drink, Neds use this simple formula:

$$\frac{\text{How fast it gits ye pished}}{\text{The price}} = \begin{array}{l}\text{value of}\\\text{bevvie}\end{array}$$

No account is normally taken
of the taste. However, if you
skived Standard Grade maths at
school, here is a guide to the most
popular bevvies.

Buckfast Tonic Wine — Alcohol 15% Vol.
Made by the Benedictine monks
of Buckfast Abbey in Devon, this
potent drink is a mainstay of Neds
across Scotland.

According to the Daily Record, during a tour of the A&E unit at Monklands Hospital, Airdrie, a Labour MP stated that, 'Buckfast is a recipe for misery and anti-social behaviour.'

Buckfast Pros:
Coming in at around £6.00 on average for a 1-litre bottle, this is a sound investment for any Ned intent on getting steamin'.

Made of glass, an empty Buckfast bottle also doubles as a handy chib.

Buckfast Cons:
There's no denying the fact that it tastes like medicine.

Broken Buckie bottles by the curbside on a Sunday morning are the most reliable indicator of a Ned infestation in the area.

White Lightning Cider --
Alcohol 7.5% Vol.

For years, this drink has been the bevvie of choice for tramps, due to its heady mix of high alcohol content and cheap price.

White Lightning Pros:
White Lightning cider comes in a handy 2-litre sized bottle that can be passed round all

your Ned pals for a swig.

At around £3.00 for a bottle, it is the cheapest by far and has the edge over its competitors.

White Lightning Cons:

I was once informed by a Ned, 'A cannae drink white lightnin' – it makes me go pure radge, ken!'

MD 20/20 — Alcohol 13.1% Vol.
MD 20/20, or 'Mad Dog', is a
fortified wine that comes in a range
of fruit flavours, such as Mango,
Lime, Strawberry and Peach.

MD 20/20 Pros:
It has a handy screw top, so you can
put the lid on and carry it around
in your tracky bottoms pocket
without the polis seeing.

The Senga will like the fruity flavours.

MD 20/20 Cons:
It is more pricey than the others at around £7.00 a bottle.

Chapter 10

Chunes

Neds have very distinctive tastes in music.

In

Dance/trance

Gangster Rap

Pop-R&B.

Out

Neds won't listen to any music
more than two years old unless
it is a remix or being sampled
by Eminem.

Neds are attracted to a song by:

* How many obscene lyrics it contains.

* How many tits and bums the music
  video contains.

* How much potential the bass has

for waking up those boring old neighbours at 3 am.

In all cases, the optimum volume for Ned chunes is when the bass causes the Vauxhall Nova it emanates from to noticeably bounce in time with the 'music'.

Chapter 11

Ned Food

Neds subsist on food with as little nutritional value as possible.

Some of their favourites are:

* Super Noodles

* Pot Noodles

* MacDonald's (AKA Macky D's)

* Burger King

* Deep-fried chocolate

* Turkey Twizzlers (what they feed
  their young)

* Any or all of the above washed down
  with plenty of full-fat Irn Bru.

The traditional Ned diet may explain some of the physical characteristics of Neds, most notably their tendency to be either unhealthily skinny or grossly fat, with the pale constitution and complexion of a bubonic plague victim.

Chapter 12

Ned Names:

What They Call Their Young

Here is a compilation of the most common Ned names.

The spelling varies (usually replacing 'i's with 'y's), but the basic names are the same.

If you are a Ned and your name

does not appear here, please do not
be offended, just send an email to
muppet@crombiejardine.com and
we will put it right... Promise!

Male

- Barry
- Bill
- Brandon
- Cal
- Craig
- Damien

Darren

Daryl

Dean

Dwayne

Dylan

Gary

Iain

Kevin

Kieran

Lance

Larry

Lee

Liam

Logan

- Malc
- Mickey
- Mikey
- Rickie
- Ronan
- Ryan
- Sean

Shane

Steve

Trev

Wayne

Will

Female

 Beckie

Bernadette

 Bianca

 Camilla

 Casey

 Cassandra

 Channel

 Chantelle

Charlene

 Charmane

 Chelsea

 Cheryl

 Coleen

 Danielle

 Diamonique

Donna

 Jade

 Jordan

 Karen

 Kylie

 Leah

 Megan

Michelle

 Monique

 Rachelle (Shell)

 Rochelle

 Sharon

 Shirley

Stacie

 Stacy-Marie

 Tammy

 Tracy

 Val

 Vicky

Chapter 13

Rangers and Celtic Neds

These Neds are similar in appearance to the run-of-the-mill Neds. However, they are usually seen sporting their team's shirt and football scarf. They may also wear a cap with their team's logo on in place of the treasured Burberry.

Football Neds are fully aware that Old Firm Rivalry is to a large extent based on sectarian divides – Rangers being the 'Protestant' team and Celtic being the 'Catholic' team – and they are always ready to yell abuse at opposing fans based on their religious affiliation. For the most part, though, this is merely an excuse to kick each other in; 99% of the Neds in question haven't been inside a church since Sunday school.

Rangers

Rangers Neds love to wave Union flags, or the Red Hand of Ulster flags around at football matches, seemingly to express their great pride in being British. This illusion is quickly dispelled when they lean across to their mate and say how they hate Celtic even more than they hate the English.

Celtic

Celtic Neds usually appear to get more drunk, more quickly than Rangers Neds after an Old Firm match, whether in celebration or commiseration.

Their football songs are usually inspired by Irish rebel songs; generally more interesting to listen to than the efforts of the Rangers Neds, which concentrate on alleged personal habits of the Pope.

Chapter 14

Ned Jokes

Q. What do you call a Senga in a
   white tracksuit?

A. The Bride.

Q. What do you call a Ned in a suit?

A. The accused.

Q. What do you say to a Ned
   in uniform?
A. 'Big Mac and fries, please.'

Q. What do you shout to a Ned
   on a bike?
A. 'Stop, thief!'

Q. What's the difference between a Senga and a sheep?

A. One's so stupid it will follow without thinking, wallow in dirt and get rutted without noticing; the other's a sheep.

Q. How does a Senga turn off the light after having sex?

A. She closes the car door.

Q. What do Neds and slinkies have in common?

A. It's fun watching them fall down some very steep stairs.

Q. If two Neds are in a car and there is no music blaring out, then who's doing the driving?

A. The polis.

Q. What are the first words of a baby Ned to its beloved single parent?

A. 'Whit ye looking at, ya muppet?'

Chapter 15

Chav / Ned Updates from around the UK

If you have enjoyed reading this book and would like to know more about Chavs and Neds then there are some great sites on the web.

By far and away the most comprehensive Chav site is:

www.chavscum.co.uk

Other sites that are worth a
look are:

www.youknowsit.co.uk

www.banburymassive.tk

www.glasgowsurvival.co.uk

www.scallycentral.com

www.hayezsquad.co.uk

www.stupidnorthernmonkey.co.uk

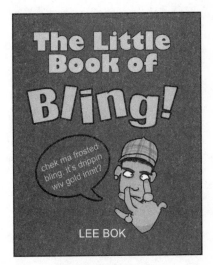

1-905102-21-6
£2.99 available now

THE LITTLE BOOK OF STUPID DRUNKS

A YEAR'S WORTH OF REAL-LIFE DRUNKEN MAYHEM FROM THE WORLD'S NEWS

CHRIS PILBEAM

1-905102-23-2

£2.99 available now

1-905102-73-9
£2.99 available Spring 2006

All Crombie Jardine books
are available from High Street
bookshops, Amazon or Bookpost
(P.O. Box 29, Douglas, Isle of Man,
IM99 1BQ. Tel: 01624 677237,
Fax: 01624 670923,
Email: bookshop@enterprise.net.
Postage and packing free
within the UK).

www.crombiejardine.com